The Club No One Wants to Join

A Heartfelt Journey Through Grieving the Loss of a Parent

Cassandra Walker-Leahy

Copyright

Copyright © 2025 by Cassandra Walker-Leahy

Dedication

For my sister and brother—

And for my best friends, Roz and Lindsay—

who all joined the club that none of us ever wanted to be part of.

This is for you.

For the love we carry,

the tears we've shared,

and the strength we've found in each other.

We didn't choose this path,

but we walk it together.

Introduction

"Let me start with a simple truth. I'm not a doctor, a therapist, or a certified anything. I'm simply a person who lost a parent."

That's it. That's my only credential for writing this book.

I didn't go to school for grief. I didn't major in loss. I didn't get a handbook the day everything fell apart. I just found myself in a moment—like you may have—where someone I loved more than words could ever express was suddenly… gone. And nothing made sense anymore.

Maybe you're there now. Maybe the loss is fresh and raw, or maybe it's been years and it still stings like it happened yesterday. Either way, I want to say this to you:

You're not alone.

There's this invisible "club" I talk about—the one nobody ever asks to join. It's called *The Loss of a Parent Club*. Membership is granted through heartbreak, through holding hands in hospital rooms, through funerals and folded flags and empty chairs at the dinner table. It's a club built on shared pain, quiet strength, and the kind of love that doesn't fade just because someone isn't physically here anymore.

This book isn't here to tell you how to grieve. I wouldn't dare. Grief isn't a checklist you complete or a stage you move through like levels in a video game. It's messy. It's unpredictable. It's different for every single one of us.

But I can share what I've learned in the hope that maybe, just maybe, something I write will make you feel a little less alone. A little more understood. A little more okay.

In the pages ahead, we'll talk about the firsts—the painful ones. We'll talk about regret and guilt and the weird things people say when they don't know what else to say. We'll talk about memory landmines and how sometimes you can feel your parent's presence when you least expect it. We'll laugh a little. We'll cry a little. But most of all, we'll honor the love that never left.

If you've lost a parent, you know: the world doesn't look the same afterward. But I promise you, life still holds beauty. There's still hope. And even though your story now includes pain, it's also full of love, resilience, and meaning.

So, take a breath. Sit with me. Let's talk about what it means to live with loss—and to carry your parent with you, always.

You ready?

Let's begin.

Chapter 1: The Day Everything Changed

It was a phone call.

6:27 AM.

Mom. Crying.

"It's your father."

My world exploded.

What?

Why?

How?

It didn't make sense. None of it did.

I remember the way my heart dropped before my brain could even catch up. You know that feeling when the ground disappears from under you and everything is suddenly loud and quiet at the same time? That was me, frozen in place, with my phone pressed to my ear and my soul suddenly cracked in half.

There wasn't time to process, only reaction. I asked the questions— *Is he okay? What happened? Are you sure?*—as if somehow, I could rewind the moment just by not accepting it. My mom's voice was the sound of pure heartbreak, and hearing it—knowing there was nothing I could do to fix it—shattered me in ways I didn't know were possible.

I don't remember getting dressed. I don't remember calling my twin sister or my brother. I don't remember grabbing my keys. I just remember driving. The longest drive of my life. My mind was racing, yet completely numb. I think I kept hoping I'd get there and it would all be a mistake. Some terrible mix-up. But deep down, I already knew.

Everything after that was a blur: the quiet sobs, the blank stares, the phone calls to other people. The way people look at you when they say, "I'm so sorry"—and they mean it, but it still doesn't feel real. And all I could think was: *How did we get here?*

If you've been there, you know.

There's a moment when life splits into **Before** and **After.**

Before the call.

Before the hospital.

Before the world felt different.

And then After.

After your heart broke.

After you said goodbye.

After you joined the club.

I didn't know it then, but that day would become a part of me. I'd carry it with me, tucked into everything I do, every decision I make, every quiet moment when I wish I could still call him, hear him, hug him.

This chapter—the beginning of loss—is the one we never want to write.

But it's also the beginning of understanding that love never leaves. It just changes form.

You might have gotten a phone call like mine. Or maybe your moment came in person, or through someone else's voice. However it happened, I'm so sorry. Truly. From one heartbroken human to another: I know that moment changes everything.

But here's the thing—I'm still here. And you are too.

We made it through *that* day.

And now, we take it one step at a time.

Chapter 2: Welcome to the Club

There's this moment after the loss settles in—not right away, maybe not for weeks or even months—when you realize you're part of something now. Something invisible, something you never asked to join.

I call it *The Club*.

The *"I've lost a parent"* club.

You won't find it on any membership list. There are no welcome emails, no T-shirts or meetups. But once you're in, you just... know.

You notice it when someone else casually mentions their parent in past tense. You see it in the way people get quiet when you say, *"My mom passed,"* or *"My dad's no longer with us."*

And if you're lucky enough to connect with someone else who's in the club? There's this unspoken understanding. A softness. A nod that says, *"Yeah, I know. Me too."*

It doesn't matter how old you were when it happened—losing a parent rips something sacred from you. You feel unanchored, like a piece of your foundation is missing. It can make you feel young again, in the most vulnerable way. Like a little kid just wanting their mom or dad to make the world okay again... but they can't. Because they're gone.

And yet, somehow, we're expected to keep going. Go to work. Pay the bills. Show up for our people. Smile at the grocery store clerk. But inside? Inside you're screaming, *"Don't you know my world has ended?"*

The thing is, grief doesn't come with a schedule. It doesn't send a heads-up text like, *"Hey, just a heads-up, I'm gonna crash into your chest tomorrow while you're at the grocery store."*

Nope. It just shows up—messy, painful, and often when you least expect it.

But here's what I want you to know: being in this club doesn't mean you're broken. **It means you loved deeply.** It means your heart was full enough to hurt this much.

There's something oddly comforting about knowing there are others who've walked this same foggy road. People who understand why you tear up during commercials. Or why certain dates on the calendar hit like a brick. People who won't tell you to *"move on"* because they know—there's no moving on, only moving forward with.

So yes, this club sucks. We didn't choose it. But we can choose how we show up in it.

We can be gentle with ourselves. We can reach out to others. We can share stories, memories, even moments of laughter when we remember something beautiful about the ones we lost.

And maybe, just maybe, we can help someone else feel a little less alone.

So yeah, welcome to the club.

You're not alone here.

Chapter 3: The Weird Things People Say

Let's talk about it.

That moment someone opens their mouth to "comfort" you after your parent dies—and what comes out makes you want to scream, cry, or both.

"They're in a better place."

"They're watching over you now."

"God needed another angel."

"At least they lived a long life."

"Everything happens for a reason."

REALLY?

Because from where I'm standing, the "better place" would be right here—**with me.**

I didn't want them to be an angel. I wanted them to be my mom. Or my dad. At my table. In my life. Not a memory.

And I know, I know… people mean well.

They really do.

But wow, sometimes the words just don't land right.

It's like people have this fear of silence, so they rush to fill it with something—anything—that sounds like comfort. But sometimes, silence is the most comforting thing. A hug. A quiet, *"I'm so sorry."* A moment where someone just sits with you and lets you fall apart.

You learn quickly after loss that not everyone is great at showing up in grief. Some disappear entirely, unsure of what to say, so they say nothing. Others throw out the classic lines because they've heard them before and figure they're what you're "supposed" to say.

But here's the thing—grief doesn't need fixing.

You're not looking for the perfect sentence to erase your pain.

You're looking to feel *seen*.

What we really want in those moments is for someone to say, *"This sucks, and I'm here for you."*

Or, *"I don't have the right words, but I'm not going anywhere."*

Simple. Honest. Human.

The truth is, death makes people uncomfortable. It reminds them of their own losses, or their own fear of losing someone. And in that discomfort, they often fumble.

You'll hear some truly strange things. You might find yourself forcing a smile when someone tells you, *"At least they're not suffering anymore,"* while you're silently thinking, *"Cool, but now I'm the one suffering."*

It's okay to feel angry. It's okay to be annoyed. It's okay to walk away from a conversation that feels like salt in the wound.

But also—try to hold onto this truth:

Most people aren't trying to hurt you.

They're just doing the best they can with what they know.

Grief makes *everyone* awkward.

And sadly, our culture doesn't exactly teach people how to show up for loss in meaningful ways. There's no grief school. No training module on how to comfort a friend whose world just collapsed. Most folks are just winging it.

So, what can we do?

We give ourselves permission to feel whatever we feel in the moment—hurt, anger, sadness, eye-rolls included.

And when we can, we show grace. Not for them, but for us. Because carrying resentment gets heavy.

And maybe one day, when someone we know loses someone they love, we'll remember how *not* to show up.

We'll remember to just say:

"I'm here. I love you. I don't have the words. But I'm not going anywhere."

And trust me—those words? They mean everything.

Chapter 4: Your Grief Is Yours

There is no "right" way to grieve. Let me say that again for the people in the back: **There. Is. No. Right. Way. To. Grieve.**

If you cried for days, good.

If you didn't cry at all, also good.

If you laughed at the funeral because your parent would've wanted you to? Beautiful.

If you couldn't even show up because it was too much? That's okay too.

Grief isn't some standardized test you pass or fail. It doesn't come with step-by-step instructions. It's not a straight line. It's a chaotic, jagged, up-and-down, forward-and-back kind of thing. And it looks different for every single person who experiences it.

Some people dive into work to stay busy.

Others can't get out of bed for a while.

Some people post tributes online.

Others keep everything private and quiet.

Neither is more valid. Neither is more "strong."

There's no gold star for how you grieve.

And yet, sometimes we carry guilt for not doing it a certain way.

Maybe you feel bad for not crying enough.

Maybe you feel guilty because you smiled at something too soon after they passed.

Or maybe you feel weird because you've cried every day for months and still can't seem to "get over it."

Here's the truth: **You don't need to "get over it."**

You just need to get through it—in your own way, in your own time.

Grief doesn't come with an expiration date. And despite what some people might tell you, it's not about "moving on." It's about **moving forward**—with your grief, with your love, with the memories you carry.

Some days will feel lighter.

Some days will hit you out of nowhere.

And some days, you'll feel a little more like yourself again—and that's not betrayal, that's healing.

You're allowed to have joy again.

You're allowed to laugh.

You're allowed to not be okay.

You're allowed to be *all of it*.

Grief doesn't ask for permission. But healing? Healing asks for patience. For compassion. For giving yourself the space to feel it all without judgment.

So this chapter is your permission slip.

To grieve the way **you** grieve.

To stop comparing.

To stop measuring.

To stop wondering if you're "doing it right."

Because if you're still breathing, still loving, still waking up and putting one foot in front of the other?

You're doing just fine.

Chapter 5: The Firsts Are the Worst

Nobody warns you about the *firsts*.

Or maybe they do—but you don't understand what they really mean until you're standing in one.

The first birthday without them.

The first Thanksgiving with that empty chair.

The first time you pick up your phone to call them... and then remember.

It's not just the big holidays or anniversaries. It's the quiet, sneaky moments that get you.

The first time you laugh really hard and immediately feel guilty.

The first time you go to their favorite restaurant and instinctively glance at the door, expecting to see them walk in.

The first time you realize: *They're not coming back.*

That's when the grief sucker punches you all over again.

The firsts are so hard because they magnify the absence. It's like shining a spotlight on the space they once filled—and that spotlight? It's blinding. It reminds you that the world keeps turning even though your world stopped.

The first time I had to celebrate a holiday without my parent, I felt like I was faking it. I smiled. I ate the food. I tried to be present for others. But inside? I was screaming. I was holding it together with metaphorical duct tape, counting the minutes until I could just... leave.

And you know what? That's okay.

If your version of getting through a "first" is showing up and barely holding it together—good job.

If your version is staying home and skipping the whole thing—also good job.

There's no right way to face these days. But I'll tell you what helped me:

Lowering the expectations.

I didn't need to feel festive. I didn't need to force joy.

I just needed to survive the day.

Sometimes that meant lighting a candle. Sometimes it meant crying in the shower. Sometimes it meant laughing at an old voicemail I'd saved just to hear their voice again.

And little by little, the "firsts" became seconds.

Still painful, but a little more familiar. A little less sharp.

They never fully stop hurting, but the sting becomes something you learn to carry instead of something that knocks you flat.

So if you're dreading an upcoming date, you're not alone.

And if you've just lived through one of those painful firsts, I see you. That took strength. That took heart. That took everything.

Be gentle with yourself.

These firsts are brutal.

But you're still here.

And that matters more than you know.

Chapter 6: Memory Landmines

Grief has this sneaky way of hiding in plain sight.

One moment, you're just living your life—running errands, scrolling your phone, folding laundry—and *bam*, it hits you. Out of nowhere. A sound, a smell, a word, a photo. Something tiny, something random… and suddenly you're right back in that ache.

I call them **memory landmines.**

You don't see them coming. You don't get a warning. You're just walking through your day and—boom—you're crying in aisle four at the grocery store because their favorite cereal is still on the shelf. Or you're watching a movie and a character says something your dad used to say, and suddenly your heart is in your throat.

Maybe it's their cologne.

Maybe it's their handwriting on an old envelope.

Maybe it's a voicemail you forgot you still had.

Or a certain song that comes on when you least expect it.

It's wild how something so small can crack you wide open.

And here's the thing: **It's normal.**

It doesn't mean you're "going backwards." It doesn't mean you're not healing. It just means that love leaves fingerprints—and those fingerprints are everywhere.

When these moments happen, you might feel like you're falling apart again. But you're not.

You're just remembering.

You're human.

You're loving them in the only way you can now—with memories.

Sometimes those landmines will make you cry.

Sometimes they'll make you laugh.

Sometimes both at the same time.

And sometimes—when you're ready—they'll even feel like little visits. Tiny reminders that say, *"Hey, I was here. I still am. You're doing okay."*

There was a time when every memory felt like a dagger to the chest. But over time, some of those daggers dulled. Some of those sharp moments softened. Now, I can look at an old photo and smile before the tears come. I can hear a song and sing along, even if my voice shakes.

That's growth. That's grief doing its strange, slow work.

So if you find yourself ambushed by emotion—whether it's a tear in the middle of a meeting or a lump in your throat on a sunny day—give yourself grace. You're not broken.

You're remembering someone who mattered.

Someone who still does.

And that… that is a beautiful kind of ache.

Chapter 7: Guilt, Regret, and All That Lingers

Grief doesn't just come with sadness.

It often drags a few friends along—*guilt, regret,* and their quiet cousin, *"what if."*

What if I had called more?

What if I had visited more often?

What if I hadn't said that one thing during that argument?

What if I had told them just one more time how much I loved them?

It's wild how fast the mind starts replaying scenes—zooming in on moments that, in hindsight, feel like missed opportunities or wrong turns. And suddenly you're carrying not just loss, but this invisible backpack full of heaviness you *think* is your fault.

But here's what I've learned, and what I want to gently remind you:

We're all human.

We love imperfectly.

We mess up.

We say things we don't mean.

We get busy. We assume there's more time.

We do the best we can… until we can't anymore.

And that's the brutal part of losing a parent. There are no more chances. No more redo button. That finality? It makes all the ordinary, everyday moments feel massive. But the truth is, your parent loved you *despite* those moments—and likely *through* them, too.

Guilt has this way of making us feel like we could've controlled the uncontrollable. Like if we had just done *this* or *that,* everything would be different.

But love is not measured in the things we regret.

It's measured in the totality of your relationship.

The hugs. The phone calls. The eye rolls. The laughter. The care.

The ordinary, messy, real-life love.

And even if things weren't perfect—especially if they weren't—you're allowed to grieve and feel pain without carrying the full weight of the "should've beens."

Regret is natural. It shows up in grief. But it doesn't get the final say.

Here's something else that helped me: writing it down.

The "I'm sorrys." The "I wish I hads."

I put them on paper, sometimes even said them out loud.

Because even if they're gone, I believe we still get to speak our hearts.

Maybe you need to say:

"I'm sorry I didn't call that night."

Or: "I wish I had understood you better."

Or even just: "Thank you for loving me."

Say it. Write it. Whisper it into the air.

You'll be surprised how healing it feels to let those words breathe.

So if you're holding guilt or regret right now, I want to offer you this:

You did enough.

You were enough.

And it's okay to let go of the rest.

You don't need to carry it forever.

Let love be louder than guilt.

Chapter 8: When the World Moves On (But You're Still Grieving)

There's this weird thing that happens after the funeral.

After the flowers wilt. After the food is put away.

After the text messages stop coming, and the world... just keeps going.

But you?

You're still grieving.

You're still waking up with that ache in your chest.

You're still reaching for your phone to call them.

You're still crying in the quiet moments, still staring at their empty chair, still trying to make sense of a world that kept turning without even slowing down for your heartbreak.

And that's the hardest part, isn't it?

The world moves on. But you're still in it.

People go back to work.

They talk about the weather.

They complain about traffic or what's trending online—and meanwhile, you're wondering how everyone else seems so *normal* when nothing feels normal to you.

It can make you feel invisible.

Or worse, like your grief has an expiration date you didn't agree to.

Maybe a few weeks go by, and someone says, *"You seem better."*

Or maybe no one says anything at all, because they think you're *fine now.*

And you want to scream:

"I'm not fine. I'm surviving. There's a difference."

Here's the truth: grief doesn't follow a timeline.

It doesn't "wrap up" after a month, or a season, or even a year.

It just… becomes part of you.

And while others may stop checking in, that doesn't mean your pain isn't valid.

It just means they haven't been where you are.

Not yet.

Or maybe they have, but they didn't know how to hold space for your pain.

Either way, let me tell you something important:

Your grief is still real. Even if the world stopped talking about it.

And you are **allowed** to keep missing them.

You are **allowed** to have hard days long after the calendar has moved on.

You are **allowed** to cry during a commercial a year later.

You are **allowed** to talk about your parent like they were just here yesterday.

Grief isn't linear. It loops. It lingers. It shows up quietly and loudly, sometimes on the same day.

So what do we do when the world moves on?

We find the ones who *don't*.

The ones who still say their name.

The ones who remember the dates that matter.

The ones who text "thinking of you today" with no explanation needed.

And when we can't find them—we become that person for ourselves.

Because your love didn't end when they died.

So neither does your grief.

You're not behind. You're not too emotional. You're not weak.

You're just human.

And you're still carrying something sacred.

Let that be enough.

Chapter 9: Talking to the Sky

I still talk to my dad.

Sometimes out loud, sometimes in my head.

Sometimes it's just a quick *"I miss you,"* whispered to no one in particular.

Other times it's a full-on conversation with the ceiling, the sky, the dashboard of my car.

And you know what? I don't care if it seems strange.

Because in those moments, he feels close.

After someone dies, the relationship doesn't just *end*.

It changes.

Sure, you can't call them. You can't hug them. You can't hear their voice respond.

But that doesn't mean the love disappears. It doesn't mean the connection is gone.

Love like that doesn't die.

It lingers. It shifts.

It finds new ways to show up.

Some people talk to their parent while they're walking. Some write letters in a journal. Some visit the grave or light a candle on their birthday. Some just close their eyes and imagine what they'd say.

There's no wrong way to keep the conversation going.

For a while, I wondered if it was "normal." Was I weird? Was I stuck in grief?

But I came to realize something important:

Talking to someone you've lost doesn't mean you're stuck. It means they mattered.

It means their presence is still a part of your life, even if their body isn't.

It means you still carry them, like a compass that whispers from time to time: *"You've got this."*

I've "talked" to my dad during big life moments—career changes, holidays, decisions I wasn't sure how to make. And I've talked to them during the small moments too—when I see something they would've loved, or when I laugh at something they used to say.

Sometimes, in the stillness, I feel him.

Not in a dramatic, spooky way. Just... a knowing.

A warmth. A moment of peace. A nudge in my gut that says, *"I'm still here."*

And maybe that's imagination. Or maybe it's something more.

But either way, I choose to believe that our love keeps the conversation alive.

So if you find yourself talking to the sky, the stars, or just into the quiet—keep going.

Say their name. Ask the question. Cry, laugh, remember.

They may not answer in words.

But they'll answer in other ways.

And your heart will know.

Chapter 10: Finding New Ways to Carry Them

There comes a moment in grief—not right away, maybe not for a long time—when you realize… they're not coming back.

And it hurts.

Like, deep-in-your-bones kind of hurt.

But eventually, you also realize something else:

You still get to carry them.

Not in the heavy, heartbreaking way that grief first shows up,

but in small, meaningful ways that feel like love instead of loss.

It starts slowly.

Maybe you start cooking their favorite recipe every year on their birthday.

Maybe you keep a photo of them in a spot that catches the light just right.

Maybe you pass on their sayings, their quirks, their stories.

Or maybe you just find yourself doing something they used to do—without even realizing it.

And suddenly, they're not just *gone*.

They're a part of how you move through the world.

Grief softens with time. Not because we forget, but because we find ways to *honor*.

To remember without falling apart every time.

Some people create traditions.

Some donate to causes their parent cared about.

Some plant trees, wear jewelry with their handwriting, or get tattoos with their parent's name.

Others simply whisper "I love you" into the wind and keep going.

For me, it's the little things.

A song. A smell. A story I tell someone new.

A quiet "you'd be proud of me" after something big.

Those are the moments where I carry him forward—not as someone I lost, but as someone I *still have*, in a different way.

You don't have to do anything grand.

You don't need a memorial bench or a scholarship fund to prove they mattered. (Though those things are beautiful too.)

Sometimes the most powerful way to carry someone is to live in a way that reflects their love.

To become the kind of person they'd be proud of.

To laugh the way they laughed.

To love the way they loved.

That's how we carry them.

That's how we keep the story going.

So if you're wondering what to do with all that love now that they're gone—this is it.

You take it with you.

You let it grow.

You let it show up in your kindness, in your courage, in your joy.

They may not be here in the way they once were.

But they're here.

Still.

Always.

Chapter 11: You're Still Here, and That Matters

If you're reading this chapter, I want you to take a moment and really let this land:

You're still here.

And that matters.

You've made it through days you didn't think you'd survive.

You've cried in parking lots, whispered "I miss you" into the air, and gotten out of bed when it felt impossible.

You've lived through grief.

And you're still living.

That's not weakness. That's not "moving on."

That's strength. That's survival. That's love finding a way forward.

You didn't choose this.

You didn't ask to join the club.

But here you are—standing, breathing, *becoming* someone who knows deep love and deep loss.

And while that may have cracked you open, it's also shown you something most people never truly understand:

How fragile life is.

How important people are.

How love doesn't end, even when life does.

You might not feel like you're "doing great."

But look at you.

Showing up.

Reading these pages.

Facing the hard stuff, one breath at a time.

That's what healing looks like.

Not perfect.

Not pretty.

But real.

And maybe—just maybe—you're starting to see that your grief isn't the whole story.

It's a chapter. A hard one, yes. But not the only one.

There's still joy to be found.

There are still memories to be made.

There are still sunsets to witness, people to love, and reasons to laugh.

And you get to take your parent with you into all of it.

Not as a shadow, but as part of the light.

So here's my hope for you:

That you give yourself grace.

That you stop trying to be "okay" and just let yourself be *you*—in whatever shape that takes today.

That you remember: You are allowed to feel it all and still keep moving.

And when the grief creeps in—because it will—you'll know:

You're not alone.

You've got company in this club.

And you've got a heart full of love that still matters.

You're still here.

And that is everything.

Bonus Chapter: What to Say (and Do) When Someone Else Loses a Parent

Once you've lost a parent, you become part of this quiet circle of people who *just get it*. And whether you like it or not, someday someone you care about will join this same club.

They'll get *that call*.

They'll stand in *that room*.

They'll stare at a wall or a casket or a calendar and wonder, *How do I live without them?*

And when that happens, you'll be the one they look to.

And you'll want to show up.

But you'll also wonder: *What do I say? What can I even do?*

Here's what I've learned:

💬 **Say less, but mean it more.**

Don't overthink the words.

You don't need a speech. You don't need to fix it.

Try this instead:

- "I'm so sorry. I love you."
- "This sucks, and I'm here."
- "I don't have the words, but I'm not going anywhere."
- "Whatever you need, I've got you."

Sometimes just saying their parent's name—*"Your mom meant so much to me"*—can feel like gold. Because when someone dies, the world gets quiet about them. People stop saying their name, and that silence can feel so lonely.

☐ Avoid the clichés.

Don't say:

- "They're in a better place." (Better than *here*? With *me*?)

- "Everything happens for a reason." (This one really hurts.)

- "At least they're not suffering."

- "God needed another angel."

Even if you believe those things, remember: *now might not be the time.* Grief isn't a logic problem—it's a heart wound. And platitudes don't help when someone is bleeding.

⏰ Do something—anything—that shows up.

Grief makes it hard to think, plan, or even eat. The best way to love someone through loss is through action.

- Drop off a meal—or just coffee.

- Venmo them enough for takeout. Trust me, it helps.

- Send a card, a text, a photo memory.

- Offer to help with errands, logistics, or sitting in silence.

Don't ask them to tell you what they need. *They don't know.*

Just show up in ways that say, *"I see you. I care."*

☐☐ Check in later. Not just now.

The days right after the loss are often a blur of activity.

But a few weeks or months later? That's when things get really quiet. That's when the grief gets loud.

Set a reminder to check in:

- On their parent's birthday.

- Around the holidays.

- Randomly, just to say: "Thinking of you today."

Those little messages matter more than you know.

🖤 Hold space without pressure.

Let them cry. Let them be angry. Let them not respond.

Just keep showing up in small, steady ways.

Sometimes, presence is the greatest gift. Not your advice. Not your wisdom. Just you—being willing to sit in the sadness with them.

Because now you know: grief isn't about saying the perfect thing.

It's about being a soft place to land when someone's world has fallen apart.

And now, you have that power.

Closing Note

If you've made it this far, thank you.

Thank you for trusting me with your heart.

Thank you for walking through these pages, even when it hurt.

Thank you for letting me sit with you in your grief, even if only for a little while.

This book was never about giving answers—because grief doesn't work like that.

It was about letting you know you're not alone in what you're feeling.

That someone out here has felt that ache, cried those tears, and survived those heavy, hollow days too.

I didn't write this book as a professional. I wrote it as a daughter.

As someone who got *that call*. As someone who had their world shaken and slowly, painfully, found solid ground again.

And if you've lost a parent, then you're part of a story that's painful—but also powerful. Because the kind of love that creates grief this deep? That's a forever kind of love.

You will carry them always.

In your memories. In your choices. In the way you live.

That love does not end—it simply changes shape.

So wherever you are in your journey—whether it's day one or year ten—I hope you'll remember this:

You're doing better than you think.

You are allowed to feel joy and sadness at the same time.

You are still worthy of love, laughter, and light.

And most of all, your grief is valid, your story matters, and **you are not alone.**

With love and deep understanding,

—Cassandra

About the Author

Cassandra Walker-Leahy is a proud Army Veteran, a member of the LGBTQ+ community, and, most of all, a deeply human soul who knows the ache of losing a parent.

She didn't write this book from a classroom or a clinical office. She wrote it from experience—from the quiet heartbreak of receiving *that* phone call, from the memories that sneak up without warning, and from the unshakable love that grief can never take away.

Cassandra is passionate about family, fiercely loyal to her friends, and believes in the healing power of stories told from the heart. She's especially grateful for her sister, brother, and best friends Roz and Lindsay—her anchors through life's hardest moments.

This is her first book, written not as an expert, but as a companion to anyone who's ever joined *"the club no one wants to be in."* Her hope is that these words make someone out there feel just a little more understood, a little more seen, and a little less alone.

She's still learning how to carry her own grief—and doing her best to walk alongside others as they carry theirs.

Printed in Dunstable, United Kingdom